Hairat

A Poetic Voyage

Swarnim

BookLeaf
Publishing
India | USA | UK

Dedication

To my Mother and Father-
For your eternal love and courage.

16. Scrub

Brush in hand, I clean-
The plates when the pile was double,
Scrubbing class lines in bubbles.

17. Two Diwalis

Purple flowers,
Marigolds in shells,
White dinner plates,
Folded napkins tell—
Seven courses,
Fairy lights that gleam,
Yet a tint of loneliness,
That's how someone's Diwali felt;

Sadabahar blooms,
Leaves afloat in bowls,
Steel plates glint,
No napkins, just souls—
Two-course meal,
One humble light,
That's how someone's Diwali's bright.

18. Mapping my country

Chaat Lucknavi,
Kashi's kachori,
Marwari dal-baati's story.

Pune's Irani chai,
Hyderabad's biryani high,
Tapri ki chai, Indori poha,
Bengaluru dosa, Chennai vada-idli's aura.

Puducherry's croissant flake,
Puri's dal sigri hard to make,
Srinagar's nadru in saffron streams,
Goa's bebinca, layered dreams.
Panchgani's strawberry cream delight,
Jamalpur's chokha, hard but light,
Gujarat's panki, soft and thin,
Poppy's pizza—modern kin.

I map my country, bite by bite,
Through knives, forks, and plates of light.

19. The Orchestra

New visitants began their symphony,
as the dawn nudged them to do so —
I ran to the nearby public park,
to catch the first seat of the beautiful show.

The magpie robins opened,
It seemed that March had ripened,
Shy creatures they are,
yet they opened the show !

I had never heard a magpie before —
their silent disposition vanished at dawn.
In blue-black and white coats,
Like gentlemen upon Papri bough,
performing with utmost dignity,
and removing all the sorrow !

Then entered the galaxy-like birds —
alacritous, and alive.
They changed the melody of the orchestra,

their voices fluttering like a beehive!

Summer birds — purple sunbirds —
their females in dull brown gowns,
their males like wizards,
in purple, mysterious coats.
The wizards sipped nectar from dog flowers,
and gave a winged acrobatic show.

Then came the Rufous treepie,
in tiger-like clothes,
his roar the loudest —
a sage in solitude,
emitting immense energy through his lore;

In orange, black, and white robes,
he caught every eye,
his stage presence strong as the morning sky !

How vibrant our guests were —
their clothes, their melodies, their grace —
The locals — Myna, Bulbul, Doves, and Pigeons —
gave room to their visitants,
listened gently, and gave them space;

The last to perform was the sun.

His rays fell majestically upon the stage,
marking the end of the show —
for he is the élan vital of this world.

I applauded.
And as I walked home,
after absorbing the symphony,
I told myself —
spring is here.

20. August

I came with wounds,
To this place in August.
A thousand different trees
Stood quietly next to us;

The sun kissed roads—
From mess to the fore;
I saw myself healing,
More and more.

I came with wounds,
To this place in August.

A thousand different birds
Warbled calmly next to us.

I saw myself begin to chirp,
A black loco,
My national flag,
And a field—

Enough to capsize my bleed,
Indeed.

Birdhouses nestled on the trees,
Porcupines wandered free,
Purple flowers adorned a gate,
Buildings merged with nature—
Not normal;
But who really cares
To be this formal?

I walked at a pace
Slower than usual;
Hence found peace
More than usual.

I healed my wounds,
Talked to peacocks, watched the ducks.
Sunflowers blossomed—
As if rebirth!

I merrily went searching for love,
Found one next door—
One with a bat and a glove.

Squirrels pushed me to countless places:
North, East, West, and South.

Each time I came back,
I loved myself more.

Could you ever be in debt to a place?
Believe it or not,
I will be—always.

21. Poem

I began to write a poem—
What a seed to be sown.
I dug through my deepest feeling,
Touched my harshest memory.

Moulded thoughts so sharply,
Delved into insecurity.

Dwelt on ideas,
Exhausted my paper.

One critic,
One in audience.

I found my poetry—
Freezing time eternally.

Little did I know,
They weren't my thoughts,
But thoughts of all;

Preface

Hairat, which means wonderment, is a collection born out of awe—of moments that felt like whispers from the universe. Each poem is a reflection of an emotion that accompanied those moments—joy, grief, gratitude—experienced in different corners of India. They subtly explore themes of classism, decolonisation and spirit of unity in diversity.

Some of these verses were written in solitude, during the long, silent days of preparing for the civil services examination, when the outer world faded and the inner one grew vast and echoing. Others emerged when I was fully immersed in the vibrant, many-layered world that India holds so tenderly in her hands.

I am, above all, a devotee of nature—her patient student. Each day, I try to learn a little more of her language, to listen to her rhythms, to translate her metaphors and analogies into words. The poems in this collection are my attempts to capture those fleeting dialogues with her, moments of hairat that remind me that wonder is the truest form of understanding.

Acknowledgements

Poems are hidden impressions in one's heart, waiting to be manifested.

I owe my deepest gratitude to my parents, Jyoti Kaushik and Gajender Kumar, who have always believed that I could do anything if I put my heart into it.

To my little brother, Kartikay Bhardwaj, who believed in me even before I believed in myself.

To my grandparents, relatives, and friends for their unwavering love and encouragement through every turn of this journey.

To my travel companion and dear friend, Shubham Patsariya, who has been my biggest critic on this journey.

To the Civil Services Examination — a path that is knowledgeable, fortitudinous, and humbling.

To IRITM, Lucknow, for offering me the space and serenity that every creator longs for.

And finally, to Nature, without whom not even a single word would have been possible.

1. The Royal Opera House

Stucco walls,
Echo Beethoven's symphony,
Marble floors,
Stage Opera's epiphany;

Greek sculptures,
Almost jive;
Victorian murals,
Quietly alive;

Reminiscent of
Art, history,
And eternal suppression;

O! My homeland,
Then comes liberation;

Stucco walls,
Now Echo Sitar ,
Marble floors,

Stage the Manganiyars;
Greek sculptures,
Hear the Bandish,
Victorian murals,
Await the qawal;

Past marries the present,
Bombay churns once again,
With cultures
Incessant.

2. Marua

"In a drenched evening of Vaishaka,
a scent lingers in my heart;
I am numb.
I seek for it,
alas! cannot find it.

In a drenched evening of Vaishaka,
I follow a Red admiral,
Aha! I find a Marua plant
and the scent I have been searching for.

In a drenched evening of Vaishaka,
my heart dances with the scent of Marua in a rhythm,
I am merged.

I asked thou,
is it the same rhythm that each thirsty
heart look'd for?

In a drenched evening of Vaishaka,

thou camest as zephyr

and whispered,

it is the same rhythm that existed from flower to flower. "

3. Jewels

Loaded with jewels, I began my holy quest,
Through shrines and silence, seeking rest.

My handkerchief of grief was lost at Kashi,
The kindly cop who heard me softly
Led me onward—to Bhimashankar fair,

Yet grief was gone, dissolved in prayer.
But there I found my necklace of greed,
Gone—taken by a priest indeed!

He smiled and pointed toward the sea,
To Rameshwaram—where I must be.
There, seagulls swooped with stealthy grace,
My anklets of anger—they did efface.

Empty-handed, weary, mild,
I reached Grishneshwar, reconciled.

With no coin left, yet heart made light,

I gave my bangles of attachment bright.

To earn a bit, I journeyed still,
To Trimbakeshwar, with humbled will.

Children laughing, full of delight,
Stole my rings of the past in play's soft light.

I stood serene, my burdens shed,
The world behind, the silence ahead.

To the place of Shunya, I made my call,
To the timeless one—the great Mahakaal.

And there I saw—the priest, the shop, the child,
All smiling, serene, reconciled.
They handed me—not trinkets old,
But a boundless bag of gleaming gold—
A treasure no thief could ever claim,
For it bore no mark, it bore no name.

4. Anymore

Long hours of work,
Do not pinch anymore;

Pain of a difficult path,
Doesn't pain anymore;

Desires of reaching the destination,
Do not emerge anymore;

Results,
Do not matter anymore.

5. Spellbound

" Floods of materiality marred my heart,
scorching heat of ignorance charred my soul,
avalanche of fear froze my nerves;

I sat wearied,
with arms empty and held towards the sky,
head bowed down,
searching for rains.

Suddenly,
I felt a drop; a drop of hope,
Then came the drizzle; drizzle of grace,
followed by downpour; downpour of love
and finally came the thundering rains.

I was terrified.
I shut my eyes.

A sudden whisper of the hustling wind
nudged me to open my eyes.

I was "spellbound"
Spellbound to see the divine's wrath
which destroyed the
floods that marred my heart,
the heat that charred my soul and
the avalanche that froze my nerve.

As tears began to flow out of joy;
the storm thundered even more as if
rejoicing with me.

My hands came down, my head
held up.
Thunderstorm receded,
so did the downpour,
then the drizzle
and finally the drop. "

6. The Humble Home

I enter a humble home,
That breathed like a nostalgic poem;

Moss-green walls,
Stoic historians of time;

Chandeliers from a bygone age,
Pichwais adorning every wall—
Countless, and quietly divine.

I step into this humble abode,
And find myself intoxicated.

A steep staircase,
Half a metre wide—
Each creak a whisper from another time.

Coloured glass in red, blue, green;
The artist waits,
Restless, unseen.

Paint splashes—each stroke in pursuit
Of the perfect Pichwai,
As if to touch the ultimate,
Or perhaps—currency.

Alas, the shackles of livelihood;
The ultimate drifts further away.

Money is the new art, I feel—
Can it still lead to the ultimate?
Or has it become the ultimate itself?

I exit the humble home,
silently.

7. If I were to

"If I were to sit
And perch
Where would I do that,

If I were to stand
And behold
Where would I do that,

If I were to lie down
And dream
Where would I do that,

If I were to pause
And reflect
Where would I do that,

If I were to awaken
And give
Where would I do that,

If I were to dive
And be lost
Where would I do that,

If I were to answer
And say
It would be in the;

Randomness;
I know that."

8. Bliss

"Beneath the buried truth
Lies the longing light
Separated from sins
Situated in sacredness"

"Unearth the unknown
Unto unending realisations
Un-speak, Un-move, Un-attach
Until the unknown is underlined"

9. Hairat in Meghalaya

Shops covered with Knup
air filled with Brett Young's music;

Feet close to football
cliff drowned in clouds;

Lagoons impostering mirrors
Police Bazaar dressed in coloniality;

Hallelujah! sings every Chapel
as sweet as their pineapples;

Roots wire into bridges
creating harmony;

Which is instantly transformed
by guitars into a symphony;

My feet pick up the tempo,
tourists join in like a rainbow;

Seven sisters roar to me
"Live life to the fullest, it is a must";

Umiam peeps with innocence and tells
don't let life slowly rust !

10. Seven persons

Seven persons on a track,
Fixing a fishplate;

Drizzle as we pass,
Sitting in a train engine;

Deep forests of Goa,
Carry the train;

Dudhsagar roars in delight,
Tells the train to stop nearby;

Seven persons on a track,
Fixing the fishplate;

Is it the persons who carry the weight of the train?
Or train carries the weight of the persons?
I wonder.

Drizzle as we pass,
Sitting in train engine;

Deep forests of Goa,
Carry the train.

11. Begging Bowl

" I am the beggar,
I came in thy world for alms,
I was given money, clothes, gold;
none filled my bowl.
Then I woke up early one day to see my bowl filled with
your grace;
filled with light;
little did I know that,
you filled my bowl everyday."

12. Philosophy

The philosophy is that there isn't any philosophy.
With each train station,
my brain expands.

With each marginal change in colour of soil,
my feet adapts.

With frequent change in dialects,
my ears rejoice.

With each moment of discomfort,
I grow like never before.

With each movement on sea shores, hills,
the mystery increases.

I sit and behold,
where next? I sit and ponder,
which of my thoughts will be challenged next.

13. Mana

Dear Mana,

You remind me of colour,
You remind me of love,
You remind me of meditation,
You remind me of joy,
You remind me of effort;

You are not just a village,
But a living soul,
Wanting to be coloured more.

14. Banoffee Pie

"I prepare
a Sunday brunch
Banoffee pie !
Tells my hunch;
Trees prepare to slumber;
It's autumn.
Cookie flirts with butter
At bottom.
Toffee enters
With grace.
Yellow bird chirps
In haste;
As if reassuring me;
I merrily pirouette;
And paint creme
On the top
Some bananas
After chop;
Gusty winds blow;
As if reminding me

To sprinkle
Chocolat all over;
I politely thank
the gusty winds;
I conclude at once,
With a silent prayer;
'I am grateful to all;
For all that has been given
And for all that was not'. "

15. Joyride in Pondy !

We ride a scooter through White town's hues,
We enter the bygone era, soon to become our muse;

At Coromandel cafe, breathing chequered floors,
we hear French chandeliers telling countless lores,

We glide past the pastel homes,
Savour a croissant for a dime or so,
Unbothered by time, we pass with subtle chime!

We park our scooter, by Le cafe,
Tourists rejoice, hands full with frappe,
Endless coconuts quench our thirst,
Here, nobody tries to be first;

We pass villages painted with Kollam to reach Auro,
plans to visit the mangroves follow!
In awe of Matri Mandir, we touch our will, followed by a
small Tato bill;

Gelato, Dosa, Risotto, Pain au chocolate;
Telescopes, watermelon juices and Frigate-
May all in the world meet such fate !

Carpe diem! We laugh and dance,
Praying to heaven for another such chance
to be happy and gay !

Not just my insecurities,
But those of many.

Not the finest syllable written,
But the truest given.

In poetry lies myself—
Yet when myself is humanity,
I shall say,
In poetry lies humanity.

www.ingramcontent.com/pod-product-compliance
Lightning Source LLC
Chambersburg PA
CBHW050950030426
42339CB00007B/373